The Touch
Of the Spirit

ANDREW GREELEY

Herder and Herder, New York

1971
HERDER   AND   HERDER   NEW   YORK
232 Madison Avenue, New York 10016

Nihil obstat: Leo J. Steady
Imprimatur: ✠ Robert F. Joyce
Burlington, July 27, 1971

Library of Congress Catalog Card Number: 78–150311
© 1971 by Herder and Herder, Inc.
Manufactured in the United States

Contents

The Spirit Indeed Is Willing . . . 9

I.
The Call of the Spirit 35
The Sense of Hope 39
Transforming Love 43
The Risking Spirit 47
The Spirit of Fantasy 51
The Liberating Spirit 35
The Dependent Spirit 59

II.
Beyond Symbols 65
The Hound of Heaven 69
The Leap of Commitment 74

Contents

The Ultimate Call   78
The Act of Trust   82
Resurrection Is Real   86

III.

The Sinfulness of Man   93
Personal Sin   98
Authentic Guilt   103
Conversion   107

IV.

The Agile Community   115
The Intimate Community   120
The Transparent Community   124
The Eschatological Community   129
Springtime Religion   134

6

The Touch of the Spirit

5 propositions that make a Xian P. 66

Real is good; indeed, that it is love. How then is the good news which Jesus came to bring of His heavenly Father's Kingdom of Love any different from any· one else's good news? I find myself wondering oc· casionally why people expect that question to be taken seriously because the difference between Chris· tian revelation and the other revelations ought to be patent. But even apart from the fact that Jesus spoke far more confidently of God's love for us, the really important difference between Christianity and other revelations is that Jesus in effect claimed that God's love for us was driving Him mad.

God's passion for His creatures is especially evi· dent in the parables which contemporary Scripture scholars agree are authentic records of the teaching of Jesus, weapons of controversy that He used in dia· logue with His opponents. For example, in the para· ble of the farmer who hired workers in the third, sixth and ninth hour, the emphasis is on the absurd generosity of the farmer. Jesus took a story that was familiar to his hearers from rabbinic teachings, but in the rabbinic story the emphasis was on the diligence of those who worked from the eleventh hour. They were portrayed as having worked so hard that they accomplished more in one hour than the other work· ers had in a full day, but in Jesus' version of the story, the emphasis is on the generosity of the farmer, an absolutely foolish and absurd generosity. Even though it may well have been true that the workers and their families would depend for their livelihood on the man bringing home a day's wage, nonetheless, they hadn't worked a full day and no farmer could expect to stay in business for long if he engaged in such bizarre generosity.

Or the parable of the shepherd with a hundred sheep who went on an absurd adventure into the mountains to hunt down one lost sheep while foolishly leaving behind the other ninety-nine. A man with a hundred sheep in Palestine was very wealthy and such behavior on the part of a wealthy man was strange, indeed, but even more strange were his actions when he returned from the search. Bad enough for him to go off on a foolish search for a lost sheep, but incredible that he should reveal his foolishness and make it even worse by calling his friends together for a party to celebrate such a trivial event as finding a lost sheep.

Similarly, the housewife compulsively spent the whole day searching in the straw of the floor of her house for a tiny coin when she should have been about her ordinary household duties. It was foolish of her to search for the coin, but utterly insane for her to try to convene a party of her friends to celebrate the discovery of the coin. Her friends must have laughed at the madness of the housewife.

In the parable of the prodigal son or, to give it its

11

proper title, the parable of the loving father, the father sits in front of the house waiting for the son to return. He sees him coming down the road and does not wait with proper dignity and decorum for the son to present himself in front of the house. He dashes down the road to meet him, scarcely permits the young man to get the beginnings of his little speech out of his mouth, throws a new robe around his shoulders, and proclaims a feast of celebration leaving the young man to wonder when, if ever, he will be given a chance to finish his carefully prepared speech.

One can go through many more of the parables of Jesus and discover the same theme—the absurd, insane generosity of God. Our God is an embarrassing sort of God. He doesn't behave with the dignity and respectability that we would normally expect of a God, won't deal with us in proper fashion. He doesn't want our magic, He doesn't want our sacrifices, He doesn't want our virtuous devotion, He doesn't want our fastings and our minute observation of rules; He wants us. And that is undignified to Him and disturbing to us for we would much prefer to have a God who is satisfied with fastings and sacrifices, a presentable, reasonable, sensible God.

It would also seem from the behavior of Jesus that the kinds of men he most preferred were those who were slightly demented in their own behevior. There was, for example, the tax collector Zacheus who having heard that there was a strange new rabbi in town did not sit in his office and agonize all afternoon whether he could take the time off to go hear the rabbi but promptly jumped up and pursued him down the road; and when he came to crowds and found that he could not see Jesus because of his short size he did not sulk away in anger at the world because of his shortness, or curse the rabbi for causing him to waste a good part of his day; he promptly climbed up a tree to get a better view of the proceedings. And then the rabbi did a strange thing. Having treed Zacheus, he informed him that quite uninvited he was going to come to his house for supper. If Zacheus had been clever and shrewd, he would have realized that letting a rabbi like that into his house could be a very dangerous procedure and would have thought of all sorts of clever reasons for saying no. But he didn't do that; he took the big risk of agreeing with the rabbi's self-invitation. And then what happened? Well, when you have a rabbi in your house, particularly one like this, you've got to make some kind of religious gesture. Poor Zacheus agreed to give back all the money he had taken and, in addition, to give half his goods to the poor. One can just imagine his neighbors shaking their heads in dismay. Poor

13

old Zacheus—such a fine businessman, such a shrewd tax collector. His only weakness was his big mouth, his spontaneous heart. He made the mistake of letting that rabbi into his life and he'd never be the same again.

Or the Samaritan leper whom Jesus had cured. His fellow lepers were of course not ungrateful for what had happened to them, but they realized that the sensible, reasonable thing to do was to perform the legal requirement of showing themselves to their priests and then seek out their friends and family and get their lives organized once again. After that, there would of course be time to thank the wonder-worker. And then they heard that the wonder-worker had been executed and they shook their heads sadly. Of course, one can understand how things like that could happen. The wonder-worker was a strange and re-markable man and said things that were bound to offend authorities. It was a shame, but understandable, that finally the authorities would have to do some-thing to him. But, would say the former leper, he once worked a miracle for me and I of course shall always be grateful to him and always honor his memory. However, the amount of time each year spent honor-ing his memory would rapidly diminish until the healed leper had practically forgotten the event. The Samaritan behaved somewhat differently. On discovering he was cured, he dashed back to spontaneously announce his faith and gratitude, and of course at that moment, Jesus had him and would certainly never let him go again. It is not just a flight of fancy to imagine that the healed Samaritan leper must have been one of the first Christians.

Or the parable of the pharisee and the publican. The pharisee was a good and virtuous man who not only kept all the rules but engaged in many acts of piety to which he was not obliged. He had structured a very neat and satisfactory relationship with God; he was giving God what he thought God wanted, and hopefully expected that God would return the favor. The publican, on the other hand, simply opened himself up by confessing his own failings and pleading for God's loving mercy. He took a risk because he was letting God into his life, escaping from the rigid structure of goods and services by which most of us try to regulate our relations with the Diety. Zacheus, the Samaritan leper, the publican in the temple all were men of openness and spontaneity. They were willing to take risks; they were willing to engage in behavior that was just a little bit mad and this is apparently what a God who is just a little bit mad Himself looks for in His followers. Zacheus, the Samaritan, the publican were Jesus' kind of people.

Commentators on the Acts of the Apostles tell us

15

that the literary form and language used to describe the pentecostal experience was designed to indicate that on that day the apostles became religious enthusiasts. The wind, the tongues of fire, the speaking in foreign languages, all were symbolic representations of the fact that now the apostles were spirited men. What happened was not so much that the Spirit came and added something to their personality that was not there; rather, the Spirit came and unlocked the spontaneous enthusiasm for the gospel which had been imprisoned in anxieties and uncertainties. Pentecost unleashed the apostles, turned them into men like Zacheus whose enthusiasm and commitment brushed aside minor obstacles.

The Spirit, then, could well be called the madness of God appealing to the madness within us. When St. Paul talks of the Spirit speaking to our spirit he can be understood as meaning God's enthusiasm communicating to our own potential enthusiasm. The Holy Spirit is the principle of multiplicity, variety, spontaneity, creativity in God. It is a manifestation of God's incurable tendency to overdo things, to shower with a superabundance of riches, to make the universe, both material and spiritual, a place of incredible and overwhelming variety. Just as the Father is the principle of unity in God, so the Spirit is the principle of multiplicity and variety. A religion without

God the Father is a religion of chaos. A religion without the Spirit is a religion of dullness. Unfortunately, Christianity as it has come down to most of us is a spiritless religion.

We have tried to budget the Holy Spirit's time, we restrict His functioning to certain organizational and legal structures and insist that He speak to us only at approved times and in approved places. Of course, under such circumstances the Spirit frequently will not appear at all because playful God of variety that He is, He does not like to be tied down by man-made restrictions. In a way it could be said that the whole history of Christianity represents an attempt to negate the saying of Jesus that the Spirit blows where He will. We have attempted to force the Spirit to blow where we will, and even though the attempt is unsuccessful, it doesn't really look like we are ready to give it up.

The Vatican Council tells us that one of the prime tasks of the bishop is to interpret the charisma; that is to say, to listen to the voices in the Christian community claiming to speak for the Spirit and to discern which ones indeed are authentic manifestations of the Spirit, and which ones do not in fact speak in the name of the Spirit. One can only observe that this task of discerning the Spirit consumes precious little time for any bishop. First of all, the organization of a church is such that the bishop doesn't really expect to hear the Spirit speaking from his people (when the Spirit speaks at all in a bishop's life, the assumption is that he will speak with the voice of the Apostolic Delegate); but even if a bishop were disposed occasionally to listen to see if he could hear the Spirit coming from the grassroots of his diocese, it is to be feared that most of the time all that he would hear would be silence.

Recently, however, there have risen voices claiming vigorously to speak for the Spirit. On the whole, it is a good thing to have concern for the Spirit once more part of the Christian life even though it is to be feared that many sincere people who believe that they have been inspirited are in fact speaking of their own spirit and not of God's holy Spirit. For enthusiasm is not the only sign of the Spirit of God even though it is an indispensable sign. Serenity, respect for reason, intelligence, tolerance of others—all of these are the indispensable signs of the presence of God's Spirit. The inspirited man, indeed, moves beyond reason and intelligence but he does not deny their importance, nor do they cease to be context for his behavior.

As *Time* magazine noted in its article on the Jesus revolution, "enthusiasm may not be the only virtue, but apathy is no virtue at all." Pure enthusiasm verging on hysteria is not much of a replacement for

18

apathy but one supposes it is at least some sort of an improvement. The misguided enthusiasts, however, are few in number, and the apathetic are many in number. Only a few seem to combine enthusiasm with intelligence, so only a few can really be considered to be speaking for God's Spirit.

The Spirit speaks to our spirit; that is to say, He works with the most creative, the most open, the most dynamic dimensions of our own personality. When that which is most enthusiastic, most visionary, most hopeful, most open, most cheerful in us is functioning (without the artificial assistance of alcohol, narcotics or marathon encounter experiences), then we can be confident that God's Spirit is at work. There is a flame within each of us, a thrust of our personality toward graciousness, fulfillment, expansiveness, generosity, a thrust of the sort that brought Zacheus to his tree near Jericho. When we give free rein to that positive, constructive force within, then we are open to the Spirit of God, and when we douse cold water on the flame of our enthusiasms and inhibit the dynamic thrust of our selfhood, then there is no way in the world that God's Spirit can get through to us.

Most of us hedge our bets. We turn off the Spirit. We refuse to take chances and we profess faith in Christianity but we live dull, drab, unexciting lives. Intellectually, we may concede that our God is a slightly daffy person, and that He much prefers slightly daffy followers, but it's a dangerous business to live that way and so, by explicit choice, we live cautious, unadventurous lives. What, after all, would happen to us if we did invite the strange rabbi over to our house for supper, or if we did come back to thank Him for His great generosity to us, or if we did simply accept His loving mercy instead of trying to deal with Him by observing all the laws and engaging in all the approved pious practice? If we did that, the mysterious rabbi and the demented God he represented would have us, and once they have us they would never let us go.

We would be caught in a mad pentecostal bugaloo, to anticipate a reference which will appear later in the book, and being caught in such a delightful dance, our feet would never stop tapping. What a silly, foolish, undignified way to act. What would people say? What would our friends and family think? What would happen to our job? Heaven protect us from an enthusiastic God!

I am not arguing that responding to the Spirit is a means of personality growth. Spirituality and psychiatry are not the same thing. All the psychiatric experience in the world will not enable a man to make a leap of faith, or to respond to an invitation of the Spirit unless and until he becomes willing to make

20

the leap, unless and until he wants to join the dance. Similarly, a response to the Spirit does not of itself automatically eliminate our emotional problems though it does give us a profound motivation for trying to resolve these problems. Therapy may facilitate the growth of the life of the Spirit, and a life of the Spirit may provide powerful motivation for a successful therapeutic experience. Psychiatry and spirituality complement each other but neither is a substitute for the other and, alas, therapy has become one of the best available excuses for not making a religious commitment. The one who enjoys playing the therapy game can talk for hours about all the reasons why he is not able "just yet" to respond to the Spirit. Of course, he never will be able to respond because he does not want to and therapy has become a rationale, a justification, an excuse for committing the sin against the Holy Spirit.

We learned in the catechisms that to sin against the Holy Spirit was a sin of despair and, as such, the unforgivable sin. But the way despair was described, it seemed like a sin that no one would commit. In fact, the sin against the Holy Spirit is committed constantly. It is the sin of refusal of graciousness, denial of the dance, the rejection of the invitation to wedding banquet, the acceptance of dull, drab, complacent, stodgy, mediocre lives when the Spirit calls us to a life of commitment, fulfillment, and religious enthusiasm. The Spirit, indeed, is willing to have us but we are not so willing to have Him, at least not today. Perhaps next week or next year, but not right now.

If necessary, we will "turn on"; we will turn on by drinking too much or by smoking pot or getting ourselves in highly charged emotional contexts, such as can be created by a cursillo experience or by an encounter group or by a pentecostal assembly. But such turning on is transitory and forced. It does not represent the organic development and enrichment of who and what we are. It is a substitute for the dance of the Spirit, a substitute which, in the final analysis, is no more spiritual than an earlier and much milder turning on amid Latin hymns, incense and emotionally charged religious oratory—perhaps with a strong strain of private revelations.

Phony emotionality no more speaks for the voice of the Spirit than did the excessive devotions to Our Lady of Fatima of a decade and a half ago. In both instances, there is a temptation for many of us to turn away from the Spirit of variety and multiplicity, of excitement, of innovation, of free-wheeling diversity and replace Him with a single magical answer that is guaranteed to work for everyone in all circumstances. The Spirit simply will not be tied down, and when

22

someone announces here the Spirit is, we have Him here, please come and see Him, they find that by the time they get us into the room where they claim to have Him, the nimble, agile Spirit will have flown the coop and will be somewhere else, perhaps laughing at our foolish notion that we could capture Him and tie Him up, but also being sad over the fact that we so misunderstood the message He brought. The Spirit did not come, and does not come, in order to provide us with magic answers or religious certainty or confidence about a new way of prayer or of personality growth. The Spirit has come to invite us to a dance, to urge us to join Him on the whirlwind which is His normal method of transportation. If we will not dance with Him, then He will dance away, perhaps to return again. Alas, many of those who claim to speak with the voice of the Spirit are desperately seeking for the certainties they lost with the passing of the old Church, trying to combine the open-ended, casual, informal characteristics of the new Church with the rigid, fixed certainties of the old. It can't be done. The Spirit is no more contained in **one** formula than He is in another and those who accept His invitation to dance either lose concern over certainties or find that they are not dancing at all.

But how can we know whether it is the Spirit or not? St. Ignatius's rules for the discernment of the

23

Spirit are as useful now as when he wrote them, but it is perhaps possible to restate some of these principles in more modern language:

1. What is the nature of our relationship with others? Are we more open, more generous, more tolerant in our dealings with others? Do they find us to be warmer, more admirable, more exciting human beings than we were before, or do they find us narrow, intolerant and rigid? Any experience of the Spirit that does not makes us seem warmer and more attractive to those who are closest to us ought to be viewed with extreme skepticism. If, in particular, we become more difficult to live with, rather than less difficult; more judgmental in our dealings with those who are most intimate with us, rather than less judgmental; more insistent that they adjust themselves to us, rather than less insistent, then we can be confident that it was not the voice of the Spirit that we heard.

2. Since the intellect is an essential part of that which is best in us, any authentic contact with the Spirit ought to lead to an increase in the respect for intelligence and not a decrease in it. The Spirit transcends reason but only because he is able to stand on reason. If our experience with a spirit leads us to ignore intellect, either our intellect or the intellect of others, then it is not the Spirit of God that is speaking to us, for if man disregards his intellect, he does not become

24

more than human; he becomes something substantially less than human and the Spirit makes us more human rather than less.

3. Does our experience of the Spirit make us more sympathetic to the varieties and diversities that exist in the world and in the Church? Are we more willing to see the advantages of variety and the usefulness of diversity? Are we better able to understand other people from within their own perspective? Or, on the contrary, do we become rigidly determined to mold others after our own image and likeness, to demand that they manifest the Spirit the same way we manifest it? Do we wish to impose our own particular form of spirituality on others? If we do, we can be sure that it is not God's Spirit who is speaking to us.

Ned O'Gorman, the poet, in a devastating phrase, describes certain Catholic radicals as "parasites, freeloading off the gospel." By that he meant in part that many of the radicals were posing and not doing anything, but he also meant that they were exclusivists claiming that their stance, and their stance only, was worthy of the title of Christian. Anyone whose experience of spirit makes him exclusivist deserves O'Gorman's stinging denunciation.

4. If it is truly God's Spirit we have encountered, we well experience greater peace. If, on the other hand, our encounter with the Spirit produces unease,

restlessness, discontent, antagonism, then it is surely not God's Spirit we have met. For while the Spirit makes us impulsive enthusiasts, it also makes us peaceful enthusiasts, men and women who are enthusiastic because they have marvelous things to share, not because they are trying to escape from something horrible.

5. A sure sign that it is God's Spirit that we have met is our decline in our need for a scapegoat. The experience of Spirit enables us to bear responsibilities for our own mistakes and take control over our own lives and therefore we no longer need to blame others for our problems and our difficulties. He who claims to have encountered the Spirit and still spends much of his time blaming others for his problems is only deceiving himself. A newspaper reporter said to me of a group of those who claim to be followers of the Spirit, that they were the meanest, nastiest people he had ever met in all his life. Beyond all doubt, God's Spirit is not present in those people.

6. On the contrary, a sure sign of the presence of the Spirit is that we become the kind of man or woman that others like to have around. They may be afraid of us, they may try to escape from us but, nonetheless, they enjoy us precisely because the Spirit has enabled us to come alive. Others will be ambivalent about men and women of the Spirit just as they were ambivalent about Jesus, and the ambivalence is

to be expected, but if others avoid us because they find us dull or rigid or creepy then, however great our enthusiasm, we still do not come from the Spirit.

7. If we have experienced the Spirit then we will never quit. We may grow tired, discouraged, weary; we may feel like giving up. But, as Father Gregory Baum says, summarizing the essence of Christianity, "We realize tomorrow will be different, and in the Spirit, rise on the morrow ready to begin again." The Spirit does not guarantee freedom from discouragement; He only guarantees that we are able to start again despite the discouragement.

8. The children of the Spirit dream big dreams and, while they are able to accept the limitations of life, they do not confuse acceptance of limitations with smallness or mediocrity. They realize that they are important and can do marvelous things. They see the Big Picture, not a small picture, and they see themselves playing a decisive role in the Big Picture. They simply cannot settle for a vision of life which says, I meet my responsibilities and I don't have time for anything else. Anyone who says that surely has not encountered God's Spirit.

9. The children of the Spirit are playful. They do not laugh at foolish things or at the wrong time, but they laugh a lot. There are some things, just a few, that they take seriously but they rarely take themselves seriously. On the contrary, they laugh more at

themselves than they do at anything else. When you are caught in the dance of the Spirit, it is impossible not to laugh at yourself because you realize how foolish you were before you joined the dance and what great, splendid fun it is now that you are dancing.

In one of the old Latin hymns to the Spirit, there was the prayer *"fove quod est frigidum,"* a phrase which is inadequately translated, "warm up that which is cold," and might be more appropriately translated, "light a fire under those icebergs." Most of us are very cold creatures, cold in our marriages, cold in our friendships, cold in our dedication to God and His Church. It is the job of the Spirit to light a fire under us; alas, so far, most of us have succeeded in putting that fire out before the thawing process had even had a chance to begin. But let it be clear that when we do so, it is ultimate free choice we are exercising. We choose to be frigid because it is so risky to be anything else.

Our big fear, of course, is what we will have to give up. What will happen to our responsibilities, to our career, to our family, to our social obligations, to our house, what will happen to our need to achieve? Will we be successful, will we ever get our work done, will we ever catch up, will we not be irresponsible if we spend all our time frolicking around

28

with the Spirit when we should be engaged in serious matters?

Work—at least that sort of work which excludes the Spirit—demands the whole of a man's being; and whether it be the obligations of a doctor, a lawyer or a housewife—when those obligations become compulsive, when they tie us down, when they dominate our life, when there is no room for festivity or fantasy, no room for playfulness, then there is surely no room for the ecstatic, the playful Spirit who is God's Spirit. Before the Spirit can work in us we must be ready to "let go," not indeed to become irrational, not to become irresponsible, but rather to give up our compulsive sin of obligations, our wearying, worrying, anxiety-ridden concern about a multitude of problems. Drugs of one sort or another are not really the answer because they are merely an artificial way of letting go and when the effect of the narcotic is worn off all that multitude of worrying little problems is back again to harass us. It is only when we deliberately and consciously give them up to encounter the Spirit that we are free to return to the Spirit whenever we wish. The search for ecstasy cannot be forced but if a man is not open to ecstasy then there is no chance of his hearing the voice of the Spirit.

At times the Spirit shouts at us, bellows, hollers, yells, screams in our ear; at other times He speaks so

29

gently that we can barely hear them. At times He whirls down the corridor of our house like a tornado; at other times He barely touches us as does a spring breeze. There are times when we can resist Him only by might and main and there are other times, more frequent perhaps, when He can be put aside with a shrug. But the Spirit is there, lurking around the corner, waiting to overwhelm us. We live floating on an ocean of grace. We have managed to stay dry only because we absolutely refuse to put even a little toe over the side of the boat. We profess to believe in God and His Holy Spirit but there is nothing we are more afraid of—not even death itself—than falling into the hands of God and being caught up in the dance of the Spirit. We pray to Him that He may renew the face of the earth. Indeed, it's fine with us that He renew the face of the earth. More power to you, Holy Spirit, go to it, Holy Spirit, renew the face of the earth. But don't try to renew me; I've got much more important things to do with my career or I've got terribly important family obligations that I must take care of first.

But the Spirit will renew the face of the earth and He may renew us in the process. He may overwhelm us with His love even when we try to escape. If we are successful in escaping we will not be able to argue on judgment day that we didn't know that there was a Spirit because He will say in effect, "What in the world did you think those great wings were that were flapping above you all your life?"

Gerard Manley Hopkins describes those great wings in his poem "God's Grandeur":

Oh, morning, at the brown brink eastward, springs—
Because the Holy Ghost over the bent
World broods with warm breast and with ah! bright
  wings.

The Holy Spirit broods over us, too. All we have to do is look up and we will see Him.

The Call of the Spirit

There are two principal reasons why we do not wish to commit ourselves to the life of the Spirit. The less important one is that we don't trust the Spirit; the more important one is that we don't trust ourselves.

On the theoretical level, we are prepared to admit the promises of the Spirit, particularly as they were made in the good news that Jesus brought us, can be believed. The good news may usually seem too good to be true but if forced into a corner we would say, for the sake of the argument at least, it probably is true. One of the reasons, however, that we are able to concede this point with some ease is that we can quickly fall back on the argument that while the good news is true in a general sort of way, it is not true *for us*.

We are not so unwary as to be trapped into arguing that the Spirit doesn't care about us. We are secretly convinced, of course, that He cares about others more than about us, in fact that He cares about us very little. But once again, if backed into a corner, we would admit that the Spirit probably does care about us at least a little bit. The problem really isn't the Spirit so much as it is us. We are prepared to concede that He will make all the proper overtures. The problem is we know that we won't be able to respond and if we crawl out on a limb by beginning to respond, by beginning to live the life of joy and enthusiasm and commitment that the Spirit demands of us, then we know that we will quickly lose our nerve, fall flat on our face, be deemed a fool and failure by all around.

So, it is much better that we don't even try. We are not up to living the life of the Spirit, we are not good enough to do it, we do not have the strength, the conviction, the will power, the energy, the emotional maturity to be spiritual men.

This perspective, then, the failure in our spiritual lives, is a failure of faith, but we refuse to believe in the Spirit because we are afraid to believe in ourselves.

We are "men of little faith" for much the same reason that St. Peter earned the title when he began to sink into the waters of the Sea of Galilee. He could not have doubted Jesus' power to keep him above the waters, because that power had been demonstrated. Peter's problem, rather, was that he did not think he was strong enough to stay on the surface of the lake.

"How absurd I am," exclaimed Peter, "what a damned fool."

All he had to do was to keep moving. It was Jesus who got him on the waters in the first place and it was Jesus who was going to keep him there if he was going to be kept there at all. How foolish of Peter to think that the issue was his own goodness or his own strength.

Precisely.

The man who doubts that he is strong enough to sustain a permanent commitment to the life of the Spirit misses the whole point of the life of the Spirit. The sustenance, if it is to come at all, is far more likely to come from the Spirit than from us or, more precisely, most of the sustenance will come from the Spirit. Our task is to leap and it is the Spirit's job to catch us; our task is to yield and it's the Spirit's job to strengthen us; our task is to make the surrender of total commitment and it's the Spirit's job to bear us up; our job is to trust and it's the Spirit's task to see that that trust does not wither; our job is to believe and to love and it's the Spirit's task to respond in such a fashion that the love and the trust grow stronger and more ecstatic the longer they continue.

Mary Magdalene recognized the Lord in the garden outside the tomb, not because she was frantically searching for Him, not because she saw Him with her eyes, certainly not because she had seen the empty tomb. She recognized Him when He spoke her name.

The Spirit is forever speaking our name but rather than hear Him we stuff our ears with cotton.

The Sense of Hope

One of the most serious offenses a man can commit is to tell another man that there is reason to hope. The Founder of our firm got Himself crucified largely because He brought good news which frightened the living daylights out of His contemporaries. Even though He patiently pointed out to them that the Kingdom of God, about which He preached, was no threat to governments of this world, He still created so much fear by His message of hope that it had to be distorted so that an excuse might be provided to do away with Him. I would argue that the principal affront of Jesus was not threatening the civil establishment; this was merely a pretext that was used to get rid of Him for what was in fact His worst offense: He brought the good news.

For all the advance we've made in understanding the quirks in the human personality, I do not believe that we have yet come to grips adequately with the strange phenomenon of human cynicism.

But it is nonetheless true that it takes a strong man to hope, strong both because there will be many strains within his personality inclined toward cynicism and because he will have to resist vast amounts of pressure from his fellow men to put aside his pernicious hopefulness.

I suspect that the root cause of cynicism is the fact of death. There's no point in getting our hopes up too high because even if everything we expect in this life comes true it's all going to end anyway. Cynicism is merely a less painful substitute for despair or, to put things even more precisely, cynicism is watered-down despair.

For, in the final analysis, man must choose between hope and despair. The vitality and spontaneity, the quest for the ultimate, the hunger for the absolute which are characteristics of the human spirit will either be frustrated or not. If they are to be frustrated then we are playing a meaningless charade and despair is the only appropriate response. If, on the other hand, there is some transcendental reality which corresponds to the longings of the human spirit, then there is cause for hope. Life is either a tragedy or a comedy at the end although, while it goes on, it's frequently a tragicomedy. Most of us are not strong enough, not self-possessed enough to make a commitment to the conviction that comedy will ultimately triumph over tragedy.

But the whole point of Christianity is that it does. We get so bogged down in endless controversies over specific doctrines that we miss this essential core of Christianity. Sometimes I think that interminable controversy over doctrinal formulations is merely a sophisticated form of cynicism. Rather than take seriously the good news that the Founder of our firm brought us, we would rather play word games over exactly what He meant in some text or other or whether a present doctrinal proposition can in fact be rooted in that text. I am not contending, heaven save us, that doctrines like papal infallibility, the Virgin Birth or even the Trinity or the Resurrection are irrelevant, but I am arguing that if we spend all our time agonizing over the exact meaning of these doctrines and turn away from the issue of hope that was the core of Jesus' good news, then we've missed the whole point of His message.

And we've done an excellent job at that for 2000 years.

If the people of God are to be a city set on the

mountain top radiating light all around it is essentially a beacon of hope which must emanate from that city. There are, I think, two principal reasons why the beacon has been pretty dim for 2000 years:

1. Cynicism on the outside has done its best to smash the beacon.

2. Cynicism on the inside has done its best to keep the light dim.

We spend so much time concerning ourselves, the papacy, the curia, the hierarchy, the theologians, due process, celibacy, birth control, and all the urgent issues that we seem to have little time for the important issues: the good news of hope.

I'm not saying that the urgent issues should be neglected, for only when they are resolved will the beacon operate with its full brilliance. But we should also realize that concern about urgent issues has been one of the most effective ploys of crypto-cynicism. Rather than hope and let our hope shine before men, we engage in controversy, we reorganize, we argue, we discuss, we write books. They are all superb ways of forgetting about the bearer of the good news.

But then, controversialists, theologians, organizers, critics and writers rarely get crucified. Prophets of hope do.

Transforming Love

The Sunday gospels we hear from St. Mark are all organized around the theme which Paul Ricoeur insists is at the very center of the Christian message. The messianic Son of Man, the great Eschatological Judge, eagerly expected by the later prophets, is the same person that the suffering servant depicted in the chapters of the second part of Isaiah. Jesus' disciples, his family, his neighbors and his enemies, each for his own reason, find it impossible to comprehend this combination. The Messiah was to be a great military conqueror. It was profoundly scandalous to suggest that he ought to be a suffering servant.

But the point Jesus tried, usually without much success, to make was that His victory was to be won precisely by becoming a suffering servant, and that those who wished to share in His victory would also have to be sharers in His suffering service. It was not merely necessary, in other words, for the cross to come before the resurrection; the cross was, in fact, the means of achieving the resurrection.

The evangelical tradition which St. Mark sets down had not yet evolved a sophisticated theology of redemption, which task was left to a later work of St. Paul, but the primitive Markan tradition is quite certain of one thing: the messianic Kingdom is a Kingdom brought into being through suffering service and sustained in its inevitable progress by continued suffering service.

This is not an easy thing to accept at any time in the history of Christianity. We ought not to be especially surprised that Jesus' contemporaries misunderstood, since we are not all that good at understanding it either. No one who has eyes to read or ears to hear could contend that there are not Christians today who see the Church as essentially a form of social messianism, and whose ideas of suffering service do not differ notably from that of the two sons of Thunder who wish to call Fire and Brimestone down in condemnation of an uncooperative village. The prophets of Christian "revolution" are only too willing to call down their own prophetic judgment on social classes and population groups who are not yet prepared to jump on the revolutionary bandwagon.

Christianity is, of course, deeply involved in the reformation of human relationships, and therefore necessarily, if indirectly, concerned with the reform of society. No one who claims to be a follower of Jesus can be indifferent to social injustice. But neither can a follower of the Jesus depicted in the gospels of St. Mark expect that a new social order is to be born by apocalyptic or cataclysmic revolutions.

Lest I be misunderstood, let me repeat once again that I am *not* saying that Christians should absent themselves from political or social action. I am merely asserting that a Christian must be aware that political and social action by itself is not going to make the world a better place to live in. It has not done so in the past, and there is no reason to think that it will do so at the present time either. The Christian, at least if he has read St. Mark, realizes that the world will be transformed ultimately by love, and if he engages in political action, it is with the intent that a more loving world will be created. The Christian, furthermore, ought to be aware that a more loving world is created rather more by the style of political and social action

45

than by its substance, by the kinds of men and women who engage in it rather than by their specific programs and policies. A Christian having read St. Mark can engage in political and social action only out of respect and love for all men, and out of a desire to bring men together in unity and harmony. There is no room in the Christian political actionist for self-righteousness, or moral superiority, or for condemnation and judgment of the integrity and sincerity of others. He must rather seek to serve all with compassion.

Our hard-nosed romantic revolutionaries easily dismiss such ideas as pious nonsense. It is not the first time that they have been so dismissed as ought to be clear to any reader of St. Mark's gospel.

The Risking Spirit

St. Paul, in a translation which has probably changed at least four times in the last five years, says, "The Spirit speaks to our spirit." It seems to me that this was an extraordinarily insightful description of the psychology of the spiritual life.

But in most traditional spirituality, the insight seems to have been missed. The Holy Spirit is seen essentially as somebody on the outside who every once in a while breaks into us in much the same way that He did on Pentecost with His howling wind and tongues of fire. But St. Paul implies that the Spirit may have a collaborator inside of us, "our spirit." It may just be then that while the Spirit cavorts around outside trying to break through our barriers, there is something inside of us trying to break out to join forces with the frolicsome Spirit.

In other words, God's Spirit works hand in hand with our spirit, that is to say, with the most healthy, powerful, creative, generous, enthusiastic and loving dimensions of our own personality.

The challenge, then, is not so much for us to seek to find the Spirit on the outside as it is to liberate the spirit in us or, to put the matter even more specifically, what we really must do is give ourself over to the spirit within us who has been pounding just as noisily on the inside of the door as God's Spirit is pounding on the outside.

There must be some kind of mystical element, or even perhaps ecstatic element, at the very core of the spiritual life. We must yield our compulsive rational control. I'm not talking about "blowing our minds" or "turning on," nor am I suggesting for a moment that this yielding of compulsive rationalistic control should be achieved by intoxicants of the traditional or more modern variety. What I am saying, rather, is that, in the final analysis, faith is a leap beyond the demonstrable, the controllable, the mundane. The life of the Spirit is the life of faith, and it is the man of faith who is able to kick open the door and let the two spirits frolic together.

48

But what would happen if we should give ourself over to the Spirit, if we should allow the best of our talents and our aspirations to come pouring out of us, if we should ride the crest of the waves of existence, if we should permit ourself to get caught up in the basic rythms of the universe and our own personality? What would happen to our job, what would happen to our family, what would happen to our social position, what would other people say, what would our neighbors, our professional colleagues think, what, for that matter, would our parish priest think, what room is there in a traditional parish even for a slight taint of mysticism?

We might not be able to work a sixty-hour week, we might not be able to be compulsive about keeping our house clean or, alternately, compulsive about keeping it messy. We might even be able to stop worrying and what in the world would happen if anxiety and grievous worry were eliminated from our lives?

I am not advocating that we join hippie communes, grow long hair and discard our clothes because I suspect that most of the hippie "freedom" and "spontaneity" are as compulsive and "unspiritual" as are the more somber activities of the squares. We need not go to the Big Sur to encounter the Spirit. In fact, if we go there what we would mainly encounter could be a rather different kind of spirit, the one which traditionally has been pictured as equipped with horns and a pitchfork. Both God's Spirit and our spirit are where we are and the action is where we choose to permit it to happen. Bizarre behavior is no guarantee that the Spirit is present and is as much an obstacle to His free operation as is the suburban commuter train. Authentic joy, hope, laughter and faith may offend some people, but because they are too attractive, not because they are too bizarre.

So there is ample reason for keeping the Spirit isolated from our spirit or for trying to find counterfeits of the Spirit which enable us to pretend that we are spiritual without involving any of the risks which freedom for the spirit is likely to create.

The Spirit of Fantasy

I sometimes quote a young poet who describes the life of the Spirit as "the pentecostal boogaloo." A whirling, twirling, dizzying dance is a fantastic image, but an appropriate one for a Spirit who is indeed the spirit of fantasy. For it is precisely through His influence over our powers of fantasy that the Spirit most effectively captures us in His mad dance.

There are, I think, three kinds of fantasy that are possible. The first kind are those that are totally unreal. We imagine ourselves to be Len Dawson, or Sophia Loren, or Cardinal Wright. No matter how much we dream about such fantasies, they will never come true. But they are generally pleasant, harmless recreation. Without them life might become unbearable, though they have little or nothing to do with any possible action in which we might engage.

The second kind of fantasy consists in dreams of "what might have been"; if things had been different, if our friends hadn't deserted us, if our boss wasn't prejudiced against us, if our spouse was more romantic, if our children had better health, if we knew what questions were going to be asked in the exam, if we could get married, if it hadn't rained on our parade. Such fantasies, while probably essential in limited amounts for most of us, are potentially far more harmful than the first sort of fantasy because they are not only an escape from reality but they are a denial of it. They are not only a temporary suspension of responsibility, but an assault on the principle of responsibility. Such fantasies say that our present life is mean and ugly and that it is other people's fault that it is that way and that other people's malice prevents us from changing it.

The third kind of fantasy deals with the possible, the things we might do if we followed our best instincts; they are dreams about the kind of person we might become if we combined realism with faith in ourselves. He who wishes to escape the pentecostal boogaloo had better beware of such fantasies for it is on dreams such as these that the old ghost thrives.

Such dreams snatch us away from the world in which we find ourselves. They stir up visions, not of a world which can never be, or of one which might have been, but rather of a world which is still very much a possibility—if we're willing to believe in it and work for it. Once we have begun to dream of those things which can be achieved, if our faith is strong enough and our efforts vigorous enough, then the old ghost is delighted because, unless we banish these dreams, he will have us, we will be caught in his dance and become whirling dervishes, sweeping through the world around us like benign tornadoes.

Fantasy, then, is essential for the life of the Spirit, that fantasy by which young men see visions and old men dream dreams—and, in this feminine age, we must insist that young women should see visions and older women should dream dreams. Visions and dreams are the very stuff out of which the world of the Spirit is created. Perhaps that is why we permit ourselves dreams and visions so rarely. We know that if they become habitual they become habit-forming and we will live not in the dull, dry, mundane world in which we find ourselves, but in a fanciful, fantastic, dizzy, squirming world in which the Spirit blows whither He will.

St. Luke's Pentecost story, we are told by Scripture scholars, is intended to convey the fact that when the apostles began to preach the good news officially and publicly they were swept up in ecstatic enthusiasm. Once you permit yourself to get caught in such enthusiasm it is terribly difficult to get uncaught because the old ghost is reluctant to let you go. And what would happen if we got caught; what would happen to our job, to our families, to our public image, to our responsibilities, our commitments, our anxieties, our fears, our cop-outs? Our dance with the Spirit might even become an exotic dance in which we will be forced to shed such unnecessary garments as fears and anxieties and compulsive responsibilities and obligations, and there we would be—a spectacle for the whole world to look at and laugh at.

There have been occasions of enthusiastic ecstasy since the original pentecostal boogaloo but they've been few and far between—at least the authentic ones. We Christians have grown most practiced at playing it cool, in hedging our bet, in not taking any risks or chances. The Spirit invites us to join the dance and we respond by saying that we'd rather sit this one out. The Spirit invites us to dream great dreams and to fashion fabulous fantasies and we say that we are too busy to do it just now.

We have learned our lesson: beware of the old ghost!

The Liberating Spirit

The difference between Bernadette Devlin and us," said a young American Catholic, "is that she had nothing to lose when she followed the prompting of the Spirit and ran for Parliament. She was not risking money, social position, respect, a successful career, because she didn't have any of these to begin with, but if we should become risk-takers and follow the promptings of the Spirit we might lose everything."

His observation was certainly accurate but there was a point I think he missed. Since her family had been rejected by the "respectable" people of her town,

Miss Devlin—unlike most upper middle-class Catholics —was free from the fear of losing respectability. As she makes quite clear in the introduction to *The Price of My Soul*, she doesn't care what people think about her. Disregard for "what people think" gives a person an immense freedom and a good deal of both mobility and agility to respond when the Spirit speaks.

Respectability, then, is a serious obstacle to the working of the spirit; for the newly well-to-do American Catholic population respectability means being as much like everyone else as one can possibly be. To the young people with whom I worked, there was no more devastating ploy from their older brothers and sisters and their parents than, "Who do you think you are?" Being ever so slightly different, responding in ever so minor a way to the prompting of the Spirit made people just a bit different from their friends, relatives and neighbors and immediately the terrifying question would be asked, "Who do you think you are?" And that would be the end of the deviation.

Because she was a social outcast, whatever sense of integrity or dignity Bernadette Devlin was able to develop (and the reader of *The Price of My Soul* will be convinced that she developed a tremendous amount of these qualities) were based on her own self-esteem and her own self valuation. Most upper middle-class Catholic Americans have rather little of such internalized self-esteem. Their perception of their own value is dependent upon the reaction of others. Their validation is rooted, not in themselves but in what others think of them. Those others will disapprove if they deviate at all from the dull limits of respectability. Any suggestions from the Spirit that there might be alternatives to the success culture of the suburban professional class is promptly repressed.

The young professional man, for example, who does not work sixty or seventy hours a week, will certainly be sanctioned for deviancy, as will his wife if she dares to have serious interests beyond the raising of her children, and college students will feel the full weight of family pressure, not merely if they become temporary hippies (though heaven knows there are few enough Catholic hippies), but even if they begin to think of careers that are somewhat different from those followed by their parents or their friends. Law, medicine, business and, for a few, even some kind of academic career—these are approved. Anything else is thought to be decidedly strange. "Who do you think you are?" In other words, the Catholic upper middle-class has laid down a strict program and a fixed set of requirements for the Spirit. As long as He functions within these limitations they have no real objection to it, but if He tries to go whither He will, then He is in deep trouble. After all, who does He think He is?

An occasional deviant will flee to Spain to frolic on

the beaches or join a commune in the Big Sur or move to Greenwich Village or Old Town and proudly proclaim that he is a nonconformist. In most instances, though, he is every bit as much a conformist as he ever was and he has merely traded in one set of limitations of the Spirit for a new set which is every bit as rigorous and, perhaps more so, despite the pretense of spontaneity and freedom.

The need for external validation of one's selfhood is powerfully rooted in the personalities of the Catholic new rich (which, if the truth be told, is most of the Catholic population). Young Catholic radicals parroting the party line are no more free to follow the promptings of the Spirit than are their suburban parents, or their brothers and sisters who have uncomplainingly jumped on the professional treadmill. It takes an immense amount of integrity, self-confidence and faith to give oneself over to the Spirit and ride the crest of the wave which He has whipped up. The poets, the prophets, the philosophers and the saints which American Catholicism needs do in fact exist, but they are still hesitating, listening on one hand to the urging of the Spirit and, on the other hand, the diabolic voices of their family and friends saying, "Who do you think you are?"

ture and the whole development of love and affection arises out of our need for one another. This point of view of religion is concerned with the basic facts of personal relationships and man's quest for a radical solution of problems that arise out of his dependent nature."

The Anglican, Mark Gibbard, argues that the most effective kind of prayer for our times begins with "reflections on experiences of wonder, joy, relief and gratitude," and argues that such reflective gratitude must include thankfulness for the benefits of science, medicine and technology. This part of reflective gratitude must also—indirectly—do something to remove the lurking, groundless fear of some that science is inimical to faith and prayer, but in this age of technology there is perhaps a danger that some people may develop a dominative frame of mind because in their daily work they have, as it were, to stand over nature and seize and apply its resources and energies for the purposes of development. But a dominative outlook, however acquired, is good neither for personal relationships nor for a life of faith and prayer.

Dependence and gratitude—how harsh those words seem to secular man. *He* has created his world. *He* has harnessed the forces of nature. *He* built the great cities, *he* has produced technological and industrial revolutions. *He* has put his fellows on the moon. *He* has done it by himself, by *his* insights and cleverness, *his* persistence, *his* scientific rigor, *his* hard work. The Russian astronauts reported finding no angels in space; even though the American astronauts read from Scripture on their voyage it was not God but American "know-how" that put them on the moon.

Yet as Peter Berger, and more recently, Langdon Gilkey have pointed out, man still feels his own contingency, his own limitations and his own desire for the ultimate. He must still have some ground on which to stand. No matter how marvelous the control he has over the forces of nature, the powers of life and death still escape his control and he knows deep in his heart that they always will. The ultimate mystery remains unanswered; secular man, happy with his little playthings, has been able to distract himself from the ultimate mystery—and the ultimate dependency—only for a little while.

But those of us who are ready to acknowledge in theory the need for dependency and the need for reflective gratitude still find it hard to pray. If anything, the mystery is more complex now than it used to be when we thought the lightning bolt was really a direct intervention of God or that the sorrowful mother novena could directly heal our sickness. Science has not done away with our need for the Ultimate but it has persuaded us that the Ultimate operates in a far more sophisticated and complex way than we would have once thought possible.

61

Or, as one scientist put it, "God knows a helluva lot of higher mathematics."

For the Christian, the challenge is even more powerful because, as Jan Peters has noted, "The true necessity of prayer lies in the Christian message itself. There is no other way in which the Christian who experiences his fundamental impotence with regard to this message can genuinely express his definite conviction about his origin and his future and the inner possibility of self-realization and authentic deliverance. Without this, the dogmatic and moral elaboration of his faith would simply become either an ideology or a form of gnosticism . . . he is never satisfied with the world as it is but always strives after the world that he wants and with a certain success, so he also constantly transcends his fundamental impotence. The religious way of doing this is by praying."

For the Christian, then, prayer is required not merely by a sense of ultimate mystery but also by a sense of ultimate mission. God indeed may be a higher mathematician (though, as the late John Courtnay Murray once remarked, "We should all be grateful that He is not a moral theologian"), but He has also manifested himself to us in love and friendship through Jesus. With this epiphany in mind, it ought to be easy for us to pray.

But Lord, teach us how.

Beyond Symbols

It is the function of religious symbols to provide man with an understanding of the *real*. As Clifford Geertz has recently pointed out, religion is "the struggle for the real." The symbols of a given religion—its creeds, its sacred traditions, its holy books, its organizational structures and, above all, its ritual devotions—provide the initiative of the religion with both a world-view and an ethos; that is to say, an explanation of Ultimate reality and a model for human life. Religious symbols, in other words, explain what God is and what man should try to be.

It is a useful exercise, I think, to try to penetrate

beyond the symbols of Christianity so as to get at the basic world-view and ethos which is at the core of Christian belief. To say that the creeds, the traditions, the organizational structures, the sacred books of Christianity are symbols is not to deny their own reality but simply to assert with St. Paul that they are "sacraments," that is to say, signs which reveal a more basic reality.

It seems to me that if one looks at the Christian symbols from the anthropological viewpoint the following assertions are at the core of the Christian world view and ethos:

1. Love is at the core of the universe. When forced to choose as to whether reality is malign or gracious, the Christian asserts that it is gracious and that the manifestation of graciousness in Jesus is the ultimate proof that Love is at the center of the universe.

2. Life triumphs over death, though only first by dying itself.

3. The most appropriate form of human relationship is friendship both because it reflects the love which is at the core of the universe and because the act of trust which friendship demands reflects the triumph of life over death.

4. Those who believe the truth of the first three propositions proclaim them to others essentially by celebrating.

5. The band of friends who celebrate Love in the

universe, the triumph of life over death, and friendship among man, and thus proclaim the good news to others, is called the Church.

I take it that anyone who admits these five propositions can claim to be a Christian and anyone who denies any of them, however admirable he may be, is not a Christian. Reality is love. Life conquers death. Man is destined for friendship. We must celebrate the good news. And the community of celebrants is the Church—these are the basic components of Christianity. When a Christian makes the great leap of faith, when he commits himself to the good news, it is to these five propositions that he commits himself in one way or another.

There are some who claim to be Christians who do not believe them, at least not deep down in their personalities, and there are others who do not think of themselves as Christians who nonetheless do believe them, and they are Christians no matter what they call themselves.

We may argue until Judgment Day over theological niceties but if such argumentation prevents us from addressing ourselves to the five critical questions to which Christianity claims to have a response then we are wasting our time.

As I have suggested before, theological debates and complaints about ecclesiastical authority are all too frequently an excuse from facing these five issues.

Someone who claims he cannot be a Christian because he does not believe in the pope or does not think that angels exist or cannot accept the Virgin Birth is missing the point completely. Does he believe in love, in life, in friendship, in celebration, in the community proclaiming good news? If he does, the other points are relatively minor. If he does not, then let him boldly assert that he thinks reality is evil, that death conquers life, that friendship is impossible and that there is nothing to proclaim or celebrate. Let him not hide behind angels and the pope and the Virgin Birth.

The Easter triduum is so overwhelmingly clear in its symbolic implication that one wonders how it can be avoided. The Last Supper ritual is an intimate meal eaten by a group of close friends, a meal which purports to reflect in its love the love that is God. The Friday and Saturday services proclaim that God's love is so powerful that He is able to assure the triumph of life over death, though only after life has opened itself in trust through death. The gospels of Easter Sunday and the days thereafter are clearly proclamation through celebration.

The Hound of Heaven

One of the five or six critical religious questions which man must always face is whether the Really Real is accessible. Good spirits and evil spirits abound in most nature religions. The gods are quite accessible and this puts a heavy burden on men for the gods are either touchy and cantankerous or absent-minded and indifferent. If they are the former, then man must be very careful to placate them. He must perform all the prescribed rituals and in the prescribed fashion. A mistake in carrying out the wishes of the gods, even if it's made accidentally and unintentionally, is likely to bring their wrath down upon us.

If, on the other hand, the gods are relatively benign, it turns out that they are also unreliable and man must constantly remind them of all the good things he's done for them so that they will not forget their obligation to protect him. In both cases, the approach is magical. One is either placating ill-tempered spirits or remonstrating with absent-minded and forgetful spirits (one notes both strains in the psalms, proving that even in a religion with a very different concept of God, the old forms of discourse did not vanish completely).

For the Greeks things were quite different. One was, in the final analysis, considerably better off if the gods stayed on Olympus and didn't meddle in human affairs because their meddling was usually capricious and arbitrary. The Really Real was on occasion accessible to man but man was better off without it. There was some possibility that at some distant date in the future the gods might reform but at the present time, so the Greeks argued, the less accessibility the better.

Another step forward is that of the deists of the seventeenth and eighteenth centuries who argued that it was blasphemous to think of God responding to human magic or meddling in human problems. He was the great architect of the universe who built the

70

machine and put it in motion but then withdrew to busy himself about other and more important projects.

Bad-tempered, forgetful, capricious or indifferent— God is indeed created in man's own image and likeness and small wonder that man has always been ambivalent about this difficult creature of his.

But at least one could be comfortable with such images of God. He could be placated or reminded or ignored. The Jewish and Christian concept of God is terrifyingly different; our God doesn't give a damn about our sacrifices and burnt offerings. He won't deal with us like an Oriental rug merchant. Indeed, he does intervene in our affairs but neither arbitrarily or capriciously. He claims to love us and to want our love in return. In the Christian tradition, not only is the Really Real accessible, He is much too accessible.

He claims that He is a jealous lover pursuing a faithless spouse and that He will not end His pursuit until we give up our infidelity and respond to His love. He claims to love us so much that He would "empty" Himself in order that He might become man and suffer for us. He claims not merely to be the eschatological Son of Man come to sit in judgment, but also the suffering servant come to offer love no matter how frequently it is rejected. When we have pondered the meaning of those images we might rather like to have back the absent-minded God or the capricious God or the indifferent God or even the ill-tempered God.

But whether we like it or not, what we have on hand is the Hound of Heaven, a hound who resolutely refuses to be thrown off the scent.

When young people reject God (and it is usually temporarily), it is not the Hound of Heaven they are rejecting, not the Son of Man turned suffering servant. It is the holdover God from the pagan religions or the natural philosophers. One is forced to wonder then why the young people do not know the Christian God for what He really is. Why do they think of Him as the great hangman in the sky instead of as the great Lover in pursuit?

I'm afraid the answer is all too simple. They don't know who He is because we haven't told them. Since we are much more comfortable ourselves with the great hangman in the sky than with the Hound of Heaven we have insisted on the old images of God and soft-pedaled or ignored Christian images. Yet, we can't seem to understand why our strategy doesn't work. Insisting that the Hound of Heaven is not the Hound of Heaven should make Him give up, shouldn't it?

I have argued before that Christianity is a revolutionary religious innovation but in no respect is it more revolutionary than in its treatment of the accessibility question. But the question has always been put in terms of what man needs to do to be accessible to God. Christianity says that is not the issue at all. The issue is rather why man runs from a God who is terrifyingly accessible.

It was much easier, alas, in the days when magic was all that was required but the Hound of Heaven doesn't want our magic. What He wants is us and, as the poet noted, He is eventually going to get us.

The Leap of Commitment

The trouble with faith is that it takes courage. I sometimes suspect that one of the reasons such a heavy emphasis was placed on the rational-assent component of faith in the old Church was that everyone was just as happy to leave faith on the level of ideas. Ecclesiastical leaders, the writers of catechisms, the snoops who reported people to the holy office, and the mysterious, faceless men who ran the holy office were delighted that faith could be reduced to measurable propositions with which one had to agree. Similarly, those young and not so young whose emotional needs could readily be served by rebeling against something were equally delighted that a series of propositions could be set up much like straw men, the knocking down of which constituted one a full-fledged, rebellious doubter.

But the game is getting harder to play on both sides. It has become obvious—as it always should have been—that while faith has an intellectual component, it is far more than a rational assent to a proposition. Faith, if it is anything at all, is a commitment of the total personality to Something Real or, even better, Some One Real. All the rational evidence in the world cannot command faith. Indeed, in the final analysis, faith can be neither proved nor disproved by rational evidence. It is a leap, an act of the total person, reason, will, emotions embracing a reality which demands total commitment and promises total satisfaction. The certainty of the act of faith is perceived fully only in the very act of faith itself. One knows that the leap of a total person from noncommitment to commitment is a valid leap only when one is in the process of making it. The truth of faith is perceived only by he who has committed himself to living the life of faith.

It must be noted, by the way, that this is true of *any* faith whether it be Marxism, scientism, psychoanalysis or bourgeois agnosticism. Every man has a faith—that is to say, every man has an ultimate rationale by which he explains the reality in which he finds himself, and no man's faith can be demonstrated by evidence the way one would demonstrate a geo-metric theorem. Faith—of whatever variety—is an act of commitment.

One may even say more, it is an act of love. The lover comprehends the full lovability of his beloved only in the act of loving. He discovers reasons for his love not before the love itself takes place but, rather, in the process of love. If he refuses to make the leap of commitment that love demands, then he will never know whether love is worthwhile or not.

There are many people who go through life keep-ing their commitments at an absolute minimum. They are the dry, sterile, emaciating personalities who are afraid to take chances—afraid to love, afraid to be-lieve—for fear that they may make a mistake. They become marvelously skillful at cynical criticism and rationalizing. They assemble powerful arguments *against* every possible faith that is recommended to them but they are quite incapable of being *for* any-thing. The only stance with which they feel com-fortable is that which comes from balancing oneself on the edge of a razor.

Or, to use the ancient American political joke, they like to be mugwumps, that is to say, birds who sit on the fence with their mug on one side and their wump on the other.

If one is to live the life of the Spirit, one must com-mit oneself to the Spirit. One must love the Spirit and that life which the Spirit radiates. One must be willing to take risks, realizing the validity of one's commitment to the Spirit will be perceived only in the act of commitment and in the continuation of that act. One can never know for certain before one tries. Thus, in the life of the Spirit there is no room for mugwumps.

The Roman Catholic Church, particularly in the present agonizing, transitional experience, counts among its members a very considerable number of mugwumps.

The Ultimate Call

A friend of mine is engaged in the new growth industry of making religious banners with bright, quasi-psychedelic mottos. She is talented and her banners move as quickly as she can make them—all, that is, but one. And what is the motto on that one? It reads, "Thank God our time is now."

Apparently those who collect such banners do not find this thought of Christopher Fry very consoling. Presumably, they would not want to be reminded of another quote from the same passage in *Sleep of Prisoners:* "The enterprise is exploration into God."

For to assert that *now* is the most exciting time in man's whole long religious quest and that we are coming to know God better than ever before is to abandon forever the escapes of cynicism and self-pity—those two favorite cop-outs of contemporary Catholics. Far better to complain about the pope and the bishops and one's own pastor than to begin an exploration into God. That might take work and it might even take faith. If faced with a choice of deepening the commitment of faith or bitching about the hierarchy, we know very well what choice we will make. After all, who needs God?

Yet Fry is right. The question of ultimate meaning is more pressing now than it has ever been. Man no longer inherits his meaning system, he chooses it. He must shop for his creed in the great supermarket of interpretative schemes. Therefore, he must choose, he must make a decision. If he wishes to be fully human, he has no choice but to begin his exploration into God. Furthermore, the new gods seem to be as dead as the old; science, technology, rationalism, liberal democracy, Marxism, psychoanalysis have not delivered on their promises to create a humanism in which man did not need the transcendent. So the question of the transcendent comes back to haunt us. It is a terribly disturbing question. Small wonder that people are not willing to be grateful that their time is now.

There are two possible answers to the question of the transcendent. The first is that grimly described by Macbeth for whom life was

> . . . a tale
> told by an idiot, full of sound and fury,
> signifying nothing.

The other is that of Teilhard de Chardin: "Something is afoot in the universe."

There is no middle ground: either something is afoot or the whole thing signifies nothing. The most important religious phenomenon of the present is that the agnostic position which refused to choose has proven a failure. Being is either gracious or malignant and each of us is compelled to make a decision as to which commitment we are going to make. Criticizing the hierarchy is much easier.

Some will argue that Macbeth's answer is more widespread today than ever before as man has become more "secularized." One is permitted to be skeptical. Neither Macbeth nor his author was a particularly secular modern man. Primitive societies had and have their share of nonbelievers; the best anthropologists of religion—men like Clifford Geertz—doubt that unbelief is any more widespread today than it was in primitive societies. What is different today is that it is out in the open and that men must now choose rather explicitly whether they are Macbeth's or Teilhard's.

Much better to moan about the pope.

I have a hunch that the principal reason for the low morale in certain sectors of the Church today is that the post-Vatican "revolution" has forced large numbers of people to face the God question, who were shielded from it by the rigid authoritarian structure of the old Church. The question is a frightening one and many find that they lack the emotional strength and resources necessary to deal with the question. Can there not be some easy middle ground between Macbeth and Père Chardin? Could not one avoid the issue by becoming, for example, a revolutionary?

The answer is no.

There have been a lot of quotations in this column. The one from Teilhard reminds me of another quote which I think ought to be quite appropriate for the convinced Christian at our transitional crisis. It is, oddly enough, from Sir Arthur Conan Doyle:

"Quick, Watson, the game's afoot and we haven't got a moment to lose."

The Act of Trust

I have been contending that at the root of Christianity is a commitment of the total human personality—that reality is gracious, that, in Teilhard's words, "Something is afoot in the universe," and that what is afoot is Love.

The matter is by no means self-evident. Most of us find ourselves very hesitant when faced with the necessity of making a commitment to the truth that Reality is Love—it seems so much easier to make the opposite commitment that reality is absurd. A good deal that passes for religious controversy and criticism is but an attempt to escape from the choice or at least to hedge one's bets. Indeed, a good deal of human life is an attempt to escape from a choice and hedge the bets.

The most obvious reason for doubting that Reality is Love is death or, as one of my agnostic colleagues put it quite succinctly, "If there is a God then He is a son of a bitch."

Why must we die? Why should a loving God or a Loving Reality impose such a horrendous obligation? The question has no easy answers though neither does the counter-question: How can something as splendid and spectacular as life ultimately be absurd?

Yet, those of us who believe in the graciousness of being and the lovingness of reality must essay some sort of answer, no matter how inadequate it may be. The Christian symbols are quite clear on the subject. We must die *in order that* we might rise again. Jesus' *if we are identified with Him* explanation to His diciples at Emaus and in the Upper Room are precise: it was necessary for the Son of Man to die *in order that* He might rise and be glorified. Death in Christian symbolism is seen not merely as a prerequisite and a prelude to life but, also, in some way or other, as the cause of life.

I have a hunch that modern psychology can indicate for us an answer. We know that the human personality expands through risk-taking. Trust is the cause of emotional growth. Trust is putting aside fears, anxieties, suspicions and defense-mechanisms.

In the act of trust we accept the graciousness and the lovingness of the other and die to our narrowness and fears. Trust is an act of commitment to the goodness of the other, a commitment which pushes us out beyond the barrier of our own fear.

The act of trust, then, is not merely a prelude to a new life, it actually causes it, because it opens up and expands our personality to the goodness of another.

I wonder if the same thing cannot be said of death. By dying, man makes the ultimate act of commitment and trust in the graciousness of reality. May it not be that only by making that act of trust is he capable of coming into contact with the full goodness and full lovingness of reality? Man can through his entire life refuse to trust, refuse to choose for life, even in the sexual relationship where the thrust of passion toward openness is so powerful. But he cannot refuse to die. He cannot refuse the choice that death forces upon him even though he has successfully avoided the choice through his whole life. Death is either an open, trusting acceptance of the graciousness of reality or a harsh, cynical, angry rejection of the reality of the absurd. Just as we cannot accept love from another human being unless we are willing to give ourself in trust to that other, so it may be that we are not able to enjoy the Ultimate Goodness of reality unless we are able to commit ourselves to it in the horrendous act of trust that is death.

Any human being who has not closed himself up completely within walls of fears and defenses, has experienced in the course of his life the death and resurrection and experience of trust, death to the old man and new life in a revivified man. We are therefore forced to ask ourselves which part of the experience is ultimate, death or new life? It may just be possible that the ultimate act of trust may be anticlimatic—at least for those who have already learned how to trust.

Resurrection Is Real

While I can't claim to be exactly an expert on the sociology of burial services I do know enough about the field to know that there has never been anything in the world quite like the new Catholic funeral liturgy.

Much of the spirit, I suspect, existed in the old funeral services but the overlay of black vestments, grim chants and the cataclysmic chords of the "Dies Irae" got all the attention while the strange blend of sadness and joy which is the essence of the Catholic funeral liturgy was easily missed.

But you can't miss it anymore. The white vestments, the chanting of the allelujah, the recitation of
the service in English all make it perfectly clear that
the Catholic burial service is in a class all by itself. It
does not ignore death and it does not try to repress
sorrow, it does not create a shadowy underworld to
which the spirit has departed. Quite the contrary, in
the midst of its sorrow and its sense of temporary loss,
it boldly and confidently proclaims its faith in resurrection, a resurrection not for a disembodied spirit,
but rather a resurrection of the total man. Death is a
goodbye, perhaps, but only a temporary one. An
anthropologist attending the old funeral liturgy might
have been intrigued by its solemnity, as indeed was
the famous social scientist W. Lloyd Warner in his
book, *The Living and the Dead,* but an anthropologist attending the new services could not help but
exclaim, "Good heavens, these people really do believe in resurrection!"

Whether we do or not is, I suppose, still the problem but the new funeral liturgy makes the challenge a
lot clearer. One cannot participate in one without
having to face very bluntly and very frankly the
question of whether one really believes in it or not.
When the message was conveyed in Latin it could be
ignored; now that it is in English and with white vestments, it is all too evident; if one believes in resurrec-

tion, the new funeral liturgies are a superb, symbolic ratification of that belief and, if one does not, then the funeral rites will seem like a cruel hoax.

And it is perhaps just as well that the challenge be presented that dramatically. The belief in resurrection is absurd; as St. Paul himself pointed out, it is a stumbling block to the Jews and folly to the Gentiles. It is just as well that we who are Christians are forced to realize occasionally how absurd this doctrine is that we have taken for granted for all our lives. It is absurd, not because it is impossible, but rather because it seems to our narrow, dull, cynical, pessimistic minds to be too good to be true. So we compromise. We don't reject it but we don't take it too seriously either. We give it lip service but we don't live our lives as though it were true, for if we really believed it there would be so much joy, so much generosity, so much energy, so much confidence, so much hope, so much enthusiasm in our life that no power on earth would be able to contain us. Our solution, therefore, has not been to disbelieve in the resurrection but, rather, to bend all our efforts to contain our enthusiasm and at this we've been quite successful.

Some of our precocious younger theologians even occasionally hint that the resurrection must be interpreted in an allegorical or symbolic sense—in an age of scientific sophistication like our own—as though scientific sophistication makes the resurrection any more absurd than it ever was. The resurrection of Jesus and His promise of resurrection for us are quite incredible; either we believe in the incredible, either we believe in that which seems too good to be true or the name Christian does not mean anything. As St. Paul quite appropriately points out, "If Christ be not risen, our faith is in vain."

But he well might have added, "If Christ be risen, and you believe it, then why don't you act like it?"

We are so good at constraining our enthusiasm, at hedging our bets, we do not wish to disbelieve in the incredible because it might, in the long run, be true. But neither do we wish to act like we believe in it because we might get ourselves out on a limb that would then be chopped off.

Or, in other words, we much prefer to be lukewarm instead of hot or cold. The Founder of our firm promised a rather unpleasant fate for the lukewarm but we're quite good at ignoring that, too.

them. They're racists, hawks, bigots, reactionaries and other odd types that offend against the current liberal fashion but we are not part of any of them. We're honest, conscientious, open-minded, forthright, loving persons. We are free from hidebound traditional legalistic convention and morality; in other words, we're confirmed in grace.

It was while reading Professor Langdon Gilkey's book, *Religion in the Scientific Future,* that I came across two paragraphs which made me realize how long it had been since I had thought about man's sinfulness.

For if man has still great difficulty in controlling himself, even when he means well, then surely we must be much more realistic about ourselves and hence more careful when we embark socially on programs designed to control ourselves and thus our destiny and ourselves through scientific knowledge. The myth, in other words, of man come of age through an increase in his knowledge is not merely an inaccurate myth theologically. Even more, it is a dangerous myth in applied science. For if man believes this, and heaven help us if he does, then he will charge ahead to control and remake himself and his whole world, justifying himself all the while by his own good intentions, and yet actually, because he knows not what he does, controlling others for his own ends. On the basis of the validity of its realistic view of man, therefore, Christian theology can utter a most helpful warning with regard to the continuing need for social and moral control over the controllers.

The Sinfulness of Man

A scientific age, which has added immensely to our understanding and to our powers, has not made us more virtuous, nor has it made the meanings of our life any more secure. Our control over ourselves and our consequent control over our own destiny seem in no wise to be more within our grasp than before. The old theological problems of the use man makes of his freedom, of his bondage to self-interest, and of the ultimate meaning of the human story have been dissolved neither by the physical nor by the life sciences. Rather they have been precisely increased by them.

Gilkey's comment is just a bit frightening: he is saying that St. Paul's classic statement of human sinfulness: "The good that I would do, I do not do; the evil that I would not do, I do," is even more dangerous in our time than it was in St. Paul's because we have more power at our disposal than men did in St. Paul's time.

Surely the opening of the 1970's hardly justifies any liberal and rationalistic optimism about the perfectability of man, for racial strife, violence, hatred, disregard for the environment are sufficient evidence that man is probably as sinful as he ever was. Our moral consciousness may have been heightened somewhat—capital punishment is being eliminated, slavery (at least of the classic variety) exists in only a few parts of the world, infanticide had gone out of fashion until very recently, but the increase in our physical and psychological power has more than exceeded whatever increase in moral consciousness there has been.

I think that we Catholics have been particularly negligent in recognizing the sinfulness of man. There were so many sins in the pre-conciliar church, all neatly catalogued, categorized and codified; there were long examinations of conscience that we were supposed to carefully work our way through in preparation for confession; we had tamed and domesticated sin and reduced it to the equivalent of the segment of time in the penalty box for an irate hockey player.

In the first flush of post-conciliar enthusiasm we began to understand once again that our God is a God of love. The Christian message is a message of love and, as the late John Courtney Murray put it, God is not a moral theologian. It was an exhilarating and liberating experience and the concept of sin was consigned to the trash can of outmoded theological categories, at least as far as we were personally concerned, though we were quite prepared to be morally outraged at other men's sins.

The juridical bookkeeping morality of the past was obviously wrong. But it was no worse than the combination of pop Freudianism and shallow "new morality" which characterizes so many of us in the post-conciliar Church. Many moral theologians have written wisely and well on sinfulness but we have been able to interpret them in such a way as to conclude that there was practically no sin in our life that couldn't be explained as a psychological hangup.

We do sin; we are free to choose; and yet if we realize how absurd was the old morality in the contention that a priest who said the words of consecration loud enough to be heard in the tenth row had committed a mortal sin, we ought to realize that it is equally absurd vigorously to denounce a moral evil and not face the fact that we are also guilty of moral evil. The Lord once advised a crowd that he who is without sin should throw the first stone. The men in the crowd walked away, none of them daring to throw a stone. It is to be feared that the Lord would receive a very different reaction in our day. Everyone in the crowd would enthusiastically pick up a stone and throw it.

Personal Sin

In one of his Essays on Satire, the late Monsignor Ronald Knox described an Oxford don who claimed to have invented the "new sin." As a punishment for this, the don became a worldwide celebrity and was harried and harassed by the mass media until he finally grew so angry that he refused to reveal what the new sin was.

Human sinfulness, as we are well aware, is notoriously unoriginal. The Oxford don's "new sin" was a put-on, and while we have developed the potentiality of doing evil far more efficiently than we did in the past, it is simply that we commit the same old sin but with far greater technological power.

But if we do not develop the new sin with each passing generation it is necessary that each generation rediscover its own sinfulness. Unfortunately, our rationalistic, optimistic, secular generation attempted to abolish sin and now is going through the painful process of rediscovering it. Hopefully, in the process of rediscovering sin we will also rediscover forgiveness for sin. Professor Langdon Gilkey remarks in his *Religion in the Scientific Future:*

In every epoch of our history, then, we need to discover not only moral standards by which we may judge ourselves and the social world we live in, but also forgiveness somewhere for what we and our world are, an assurance of the ability to accept ourselves and our world, even in the ambiguity that we know to characterize them when we are aware of the truth. For only thus are we enabled to go on with our worldly work for a better and juster world than we now have. And in order to do *that*, we need to have a faith that something works for good, even beyond and within the mess that we men have made and will continue to make; we need an intelligible ground for hope, a credible "myth" that does not lie to us about ourselves and our future. Finally, if life is in this way made up of ambiguity and frequent conflict, we need to have an urge for reconciliation, with the others whom we have injured and with ourselves too. All of this points beyond the scope and capabilities of our own knowledge and of our own moral powers to the deeper sources of both, the God who is creative of our astounding capacities, who judges our waywardness, and who accepts our repentance; who works in the midst of our evil as well as of our good to further his purposes and fulfil his promises; and who call us to reconciliation so that we may start again on his and our work for a better and more humane future.

The vast new powers of science do not, in the end, make religious faith and commitment irrelevant; they make them more necessary than ever. And they make of the utmost importance the understanding and the use of the deeper symbols expressive of the real issues and so the realistic possibilities of man's destiny—the symbols of man's potentialities and nature as the image of God, of his waywardness as fallen from grace; of the judgment, the mercy, and the promise of God. For only on these terms can the mystery, the risk, and the hopes of the destiny of a scientific culture be comprehended and borne.

"The image of God," "fallen from grace," "judgment," "mercy"—these are all extremely old-fashioned words. One would have expected to discover them in the spiritual manuals of the past but not in a book by a man who is rapidly becoming the most important theologian of the seventies.

Yet Gilkey's point is of critical importance for the seventies: only a man who discovers his own sinfulness is capable also of discovering forgiveness, and only a man who experiences the need to be forgiven also experiences the obligation to forgive others.

And we are so loathe to forgive others—the young

100

will not forgive the old, the old will not forgive the young; the poor will not forgive the rich, and the rich will not forgive the poor; the black will not forgive the white, and the white will not forgive the black. Indeed, not only men and women to be blamed for their own guilt but also for the guilt of their parents or anyone who is of the same color or social class or religion or age. All whites, all blacks, all young, all old, all rich, all poor, all Jews, all Christians —they are all guilty of the sins that have been committed by some of their numbers. One would have thought that tribal guilt would have vanished from the race with the fall of Adolf Hitler but it turns out that some of the most liberal and progressive among us have resurrected the principle of tribal guilt and are using it with reckless abandon—usually, of course, against members of other tribes.

While there are no new sins there are certain kinds of sinfulness that are particularly tempting to members of certain groups. The young are tempted to rash judgment, the old to complacency, the intellectual to pride and arrogance, the liberal to incredible self-righteousness, but there is one kind of sin that seems to underpin all of the others, a sinfulness equally available to the rich and the poor, the young and the old, the liberal and the conservative: it is the sin of judging others' sinfulness and ignoring our own, or as the Lord said, seeing the splinter in the other's eye and ignoring the beam in ours. It is an easy sin at any time but it is especially easy in an era when some of our most glib young theologians are urging us to a theology of class conflict and of revolution, a theology which almost demands that we make moral judgments about the evil of others, a theology which urges us to harshness, destruction and violence instead of compassion, affection and sympathy, which urges us to tear down instead of build up, which urges us to destroy our enemies instead of loving them.

To the extent that we commit the sin of dwelling on the other's splinter and ignoring our own beam, we are quite incapable of experiencing either sinfulness or the forgiveness which Professor Gilkey describes so beautifully. It is to be feared that the Lord's verdict on us will be rather harsh: we have judged and we will be judged.

Authentic Guilt

When one is reflecting on the gloomy business of sin, one cannot escape the equally gloomy business of guilt; the sinner is guilty and he must expiate his guilt. Unfortunately for us, there are a number of different kinds of guilt and they are easily confused especially since it is frequently much to our benefit to confuse them.

The two that I wish to consider right now are neurotic guilt and moral guilt. ~~Moral~~ *Neurotic* guilt is the free-floating anxiety that lurks in our personality as the result of unresolved conflicts with our parents. It leads to obsessiveness, compulsiveness, scruples and a vast variety of other self-defeating, self-punishing and self-hating behavior. Moral guilt, on the other hand, is the relatively neurosis-free realization that we have done wrong and are a sinner in the eyes of God and man.

The thing about neurotic guilt is that while it is painful it's not nearly as painful as authentic moral guilt. The scrupulous person who drives confessors crazy with his neurotic anxieties is thereby excused from facing the real duties and responsibilities of life. The rigid, compulsive moralizer who, in pre-conciliar days, used to present in the confessional the most detailed accounts of the most minute peccadillos was thereby freed from any obligation of asking whether there was really any openness and love and trust in his relationship with others. Neurosis, though not perceived as such, was a marvelous excuse for running away from the real world of love and hatred, hope and discouragement, joy and sorrow.

But in the post-conciliar Church we have found a new and equally marvelous confusion, too. We are now capable of making explicit use of neurosis to excuse our guilt. We dismiss every feeling of guilt and moral responsibility we experience as arising from our neurosis; the very fact that we can persuade ourself that our guilt is neurotic dispenses us from any further responsible behavior in the area claimed to be effected by the neurosis. It's a little more complicated and devious than the cop-out of the scrupulous compulsive but it just as effectively freezes moral responsibility.

Have I made a commitment to somebody that now I do not want to honor? Well, I'm sorry about it but that somebody has become a father-figure or a sibling surrogate and hence my commitment to him is neurotic and therefore I don't have to honor it. Have I assumed a responsibility I do not want to discharge? Alas, that responsibility has got caught up with my guilt feelings and I am unable therefore to do it spontaneously and creatively. It's no longer "my own thing" and to do it now would be to violate my "life project."

Do I have a talent which I ought to develop which would require hard work? Well, of course I can't do it because if I once get involved in hard work sharpening that talent I would be doing it to win the approval and acceptance of parent figures and that would be altogether bad, so therefore the best bet is for me not even to try.

Does it seem likely that I am only half-educated and that I pontificate on a good number of things that I don't know anything about? Obviously, then, I require more education and training or at least far more intensive reading, but this would bring back unhappy memories of the narrowness and rigidity of my school days and, rather than risk those unhappy memories, it would be much better for me to continue to be half-educated.

The game can be played indefinitely. It must be admitted that it is a much more pleasant game than that of the scrupulous compulsive—the compulsive finds life extremely unpleasant, whereas the clever and witty fellow who is so conscious of his own neurotic tendencies has an extraordinarily easy life. As a matter of fact, there is *no* obligation he can't get out of with a perfectly convincing and persuasive explanation of how he is a prisoner of the guilt feelings of his past.

In the last meditation we quoted Professor Langdon Gilkey on the relationship between sinfulness and the need for forgiveness, but the last thing many people want is forgiveness, for, if they were capable of forgiveness, then it would follow that they were also capable of guilt—real moral guilt for ignoring their obligations to others and the best that is oneself. And if those occasional gnawing pangs of conscience were authentic guilt instead of neurotic guilt they might have to dramatically alter their lives.

And then what would they have left to discuss with their therapy groups?

Conversion

In the marvelous, sin-free world of post-conciliar Catholics there is no need for *conversion*. We may of course undergo change, indeed dramatic change in some kind of group experience. This change may make us remarkably skillful at analyzing the motives of others—and of course compelling others to listen to these skillful analyses. But such changes are not "conversions." They represent a discovery of a new and undreamed of power inside ourselves, a new awareness about the meaning of human relationships and a new clarity about the way men ought to live. We turn away from past habits not because they were sinful but because they were based on ignorance and a lack of "sensitivity."

As I have said before, group experiences can be terribly important to peoples' lives. Indeed, long years of work with one Christian group which I suppose would now be called a "commune" has convinced me of the importance and the limitations of group dynamics.

Furthermore, our increasing sophistication by group processes may very well facilitate authentic "conversion." Unfortunately, shallow and superficial dynamics techniques can produce a counterfeit of "conversion"—a phenomenon in which a member of the group breaks down and reveals "hidden secrets" about himself, much to the delight of the other members of the group. While such "revelations" may appeal to the voyeuristic tendencies of the group and the exhibitionistic tendencies of the self-revealer they need not be psychologically healthy and may have absolutely nothing to do with a "conversion," that is, an authentic and profound change in one's life. I do not deny that conversions can happen in group circumstances, nor do I deny that in fact some do occur. All I am saying is that they do not occur automatically and that many instances of what purport to be "conversion" are a rather unhealthy example of psychological game-playing.

But "conversions" we still must have. Indeed, in the

healthy psychological, to say nothing of the healthy spiritual life, "conversions" are absolutely indispensable.

For in a "conversion" one returns to "go" and starts all over again. One makes a new beginning. One acknowledges the mistakes, the blunders, the selfishness, the narrowness, the harshness, the rigidity, the timidity, the suspicion, the distrust, the anger, the hatred, the malice of one's past. One faces realistically the reasons for all such ugliness and evil and one resolves sincerely, but with realistic humility, that one is going to do better—with of course the full awareness that in the not too distant future another "conversion" is going to be necessary.

One of the great harms that came from the mechanical and juridical approach to the sacrament of penance in by-gone years is that the "conversion" which was supposed to accompany our weekly confession became routine and conventional. We asserted constantly, glibly and frequently meaninglessly that we were going to "amend our life, amen," but thirty seconds after we had slipped out of the confessional, rattled off the penance and escaped from the church, the amendment of our life was gone from our minds. The magic rituals had been performed, the magic words had been said, a pious hope had been expressed, and now we must get to the local theater before the second feature began.

"Conversion," to be meaningful, requires a combination of sorrow and hopefulness—sorrow over the mess we've made of things in the past and hopefulness about our ability to do better in the future—a hopefulness which is not weakened by the honest realization that if we do in fact manage to do "better" it is very likely only to be slightly better.

If the old confessional "purpose of amendment" so easily became mechanical and routine, our new optimism about man and our new—generally shallow—understanding of depth psychology seems to eliminate the need for "conversion" experiences. We may "turn on" psychologically in group discussion or in folk-music liturgy, but this does not necessitate our facing plainly the ugliness that we have lived and reducing somewhat the level of that ugliness. The hell fire and brimstone, the devil and sin sermons from the old retreats are gone; most of them will scarcely be missed. But, if in the process we ignore the dark, sinful side of the human condition and of our human personality, we are merely exchanging one extreme for another.

The new—and allegedly final—liturgical revision has a penitential service at its very beginning. It is a splendid opportunity to remind ourselves of the remaining darkness that still infects our selfhood. Sin does, after all, remain in the post-conciliar Church; even if we are expected to acknowledge it before

Mass begins. Whether such acknowledgement represents a genuine, if rather brief "conversion" for those of us who mouth the words remains to be seen.

How foolish of John the Baptist to announce that one should do penance for one's sins because the Kingdom of God was at hand.

The Agile Community

Much recent theological writing suggests that it is the "local community" rather than the diocese that is the basic unit in the structure of the Church. In the New Testament there was practically no distinction between the two, but according to contemporary theologians the thrust of the New Testament ecclesiology is that the Church is to be found wherever there is a local worshipping community. This obviously means the "parish" more than it does a diocese, the way the diocese is organized today. Paris, New York, Chicago, Rome are worshipping communities only when the words are stretched beyond all ordinary meaning.

In such a view of things the rest of the structure of the Church exists to maintain unity and communication among the local communities, to remind them of their obligation not to isolate themselves from other communities, and to keep them in communication with the rest of the Church.

It is characteristic, I suppose, of the strange and illogical times in which we live that statements like those in the previous paragraph will be read as weakening the power and the responsibility of the bishops and the pope who preside over the organizational structure that transcends the parochial community. In fact, however, such a theory of the Church strengthens the responsibility and obligations of the hierarchical structure, and makes it more important rather than less important.

But my purpose is not to try to persuade either the left or the right that a hierarchical structure is indispensable; rather it is to make some comments about what qualities should characterize the Church as a local community. (And local need not be read to mean "circumscribed by particular territorial boundaries"; the whole history of Christianity shows that the local worshipping community frequently has not been territorial. The so-called "floating parish" or "commune" are but the most recent in a long line of nonterritorial communities of which the immediate ancestor was the national parish of the ethnic immigrant groups.)

The first quality that must be found in a local community is one that I call "agility." By this I mean a characteristic of the community that makes it flexible, mobile and readily disposed to respond to the promptings of the Spirit. The Christian community must, as Jesus makes clear to his apostles in the New Testament, be ready to travel light and to play it by ear—with of course the ear cocked to the inspirations of the Spirit. It must not permit itself to be bogged down by either physical or organizational structures. It exists to proclaim good news, and it must be ready to move and to move quickly when there is a new opportunity to proclaim the good news.

In some quarters an instantaneous reaction is to say that therefore the parish must not own any buildings and particularly must get rid of its schools. (What a splendid scapegoat the school has been! I wonder what a certain brand of Catholics would do if they did not have the school to attack.) That there will be in the evolving Church, some parochial communities which will have no physical structures and only modest organizational structures, I do not doubt, but it does not follow that they will be any more agile than many of our large urban parishes—though heaven knows most of them aren't agile either. Physical and organizational structures can facilitate agility, particularly when there is enough imagination and creativity present in the leadership. Pan American Airlines has a good deal more agility than a suburban car pool despite the fact that its physical possessions and its organizational complexity are much greater. What is required, of course, is that means do not become ends. Unfortunately, the "physical plant" of the parish has all too frequently become an end unto itself, and the ability to move quickly or even to move at all has not merely been lost, it has come to be viewed as not worth having.

Most American parishes, I fear, would not score very well on any scale of agility. They are both musclebound and tradition-bound. The old monsignorial arguments, "We've never done it that way," or, "We've always done it that way," are perhaps heard a little less frequently today than they were fifteen years ago, but the definition of problems, the styles of behavior, traditional procedures and even the influential people in most American parishes are stodgy to the point of being inert. Nor is there any particular reason to think that the introduction of the parish council automatically solves this problem, since frequently it becomes just one more veto group that interferes with the community's ability to respond quickly to the inspiration of the Spirit and to move rapidly when the time has come to move. Perhaps the most important factor in making the parish agile would be in the priest who leads it; but while I suppose that the clergy today are more agile than the laity, they are still not very agile; partly because of their own identity problems and partly because they lack either the convictions or the rhetoric to stir up the Spirit in their parishioners.

One would not be justified in giving in to despair about the parochial community. Traditional parishes are far more likely to display the beginnings of agility than they have at any time in the last several hundred years. The new unofficial parochial communities that are emerging—I am sure under the inspiration of the Holy Spirit—are frequently very agile (though not always so as anyone who has dealt with them must realize). Nevertheless, if one reads the instructions of Jesus to His apostles in the sixth chapter of St. Mark, one realizes how far we have to go before we can evidence *that* kind of agility.

The Intimate Community

The liturgical revival certainly has not been a failure, but neither has it produced the splendid effects that were anticipated, and it has left the Catholic population vaguely confused if still generally sympathetic. A number of things went wrong, of course. The gradual changes of the past six years have given the impression that the Church leadership was rather uncertain as to what it was about in liturgical reform, and was "fiddling" with the Mass. By and large the programs of instruction on liturgical reform have been high-flown and a priori and monstrously ineffective—as indeed is everything else in which the so-called "religious educators" have had a hand. The rubricists have fought a persistent rearguard action, trying to impose the same horrendous atmosphere of juridical rigidity on the new liturgy as they had imposed on the old.

But the real problem with the liturgical reform has not been the inevitable mistakes that would be made in carrying out any reform. The real problem has been the assumption in the constitution itself that large urban parishes are appropriate places for anything but "audience" involvement in worship. You simply cannot have a worshipping *community* of 5000 or even 3000 people. The failure of the liturgical renewal to live up to the great expectations everyone had for it points out, I think, a second quality of the local Christian community: it must be *intimate.* One need only look at the model of the Last Supper to see that the first eucharistic banquet was celebrated by a small group of friends. And both the family meal symbol and the discourse St. John reports from that banquet indicate that it was conceived as an intimate affair. The Passover meal was not in fact a Passover unless it was a gathering of a *family*, and Jesus assured His followers that they were no longer servants but friends. A parish of 5000 people, no matter how admirable it may be, can scarely be called a community of friends unless the word "friend" loses most of its meaning; nor can it be called a family unless the word "family" is distorted beyond all recognition.

The essence of the Christian relationship is love. "By this shall all men know that you are my disciples; that you have love for one another." Indeed, a love modeled after the love Jesus has had for us. The kind of profound intimate love that Jesus wishes His disciples to model their lives after is simply not the sort of thing that can be experienced in a large amorphous congregation in which people do not even know each other. It is, I suppose, charming to shake hands with the stranger next to us in church at communion time and say, "Peace," but it doesn't mean very much, and indeed is almost a rather foolish gesture if we don't know the man any better than the man who sits next to us on the subway or the bus as we go to work in the morning. It's nice to say hello to him, one supposes, but it is foolish to think that saying hello creates a deep and meaningful relationship; a relationship by which others can judge us to be the followers of Jesus of Nazareth.

Local communities of Christians as they now exist in the United States are much too big. Too big for effective worship, too big for effective social support of apostolic action and too big to be models of the relationship between Jesus and His apostles which, I would imagine no one would deny, is the goal of all Christian communities.

There are all kinds of social and historical reasons explaining the large urban parish. One is not criticizing the men who created them or who administered them, and who brought some sense of Christian community to them despite almost insurmountable obstacles. Nor is one expecting that they are going to collapse overnight. Nevertheless, from the point of view of the goals in the constitution on the liturgy and of the imagery of the New Testament, large urban parishes are grotesque. Until we find some effective way of reconstituting them as collections of much smaller communities, we are not going to be honoring the Christian ideal.

For ours is a religion of love, intimate, passionate love; love that Jesus displayed for His apostles at the Last Supper. You cannot have feelings of intimate and passionate love for people you do not know, and you cannot be expected to know 5000 or 10,000 or 20,000 people. Until our Christian communities become much more intimate, they will be very inadequate manifestations of the love of Jesus for us.

The Transparent Community

There has been much talk lately about the need for "charismatic" leadership. The charismatic leader is one whose commitments and convictions are transparent; that is to say, the kind of person he is and the life he lives leave us in no doubt as to where he stands and where he is going.

But the word "charisma," like most words in a highly verbal society like our own, has quickly degenerated. Not so long ago I saw an advertisement in the *New York Times* announcing that the latest fashion in crochet dresses was "charismatic," to which one ecclesiastical wag I know commented, "What the *Times*'s ad had obviously meant was that the dresses were transparent."

Whether dresses are transparent or not may be an extremely important question for the spiritual life; it may even be that the answer is not quite as obvious as it was a decade ago; but there is no possible debate about the need for the Christian community to be transparent. Not only must it be, as we have said in previous columns, "agile" and "intimate"; it must be transparent. He who looks at the local Christian community from the outside must be able to tell instantaneously where it stands and in what direction it's going. Jesus left no room for any compromise: "By this shall all men know that you are my disciples: that you have love for one another." The witness bearing of the Church, the shedding of light from the mountaintop is a relational activity. We bear witness, we shed light precisely by the quality of the relationships that exist among us. If the local Christian community, which is the fundamental reality in the Church, is not transparent; if it does not display in the quality of its relationships the love which Jesus insists must be characteristic of His followers, then it can lay no legitimate claim to the title of Christian.

It is in this transparency of the Christian community that we also find the root of its social-action orientation. For the Christian community must also show forth its conviction that Jesus is served in the least of the brothers, and that whatever we do to the least of the brothers we do to Him. Thus, a Christian community that is turned in upon itself and has no concern for the world outside is a contradiction in terms; it has lost its transparency and become opaque. Those who look at it see not the love which ought to characterize the followers of Jesus, but narrowness and selfishness.

Because it is transparent, the Christian community must also have two other qualities. It must be both "prophetic" and "healing"; that is to say, it must challenge the complacency of the world around it, and it must heal the wounds in that world. It stirs men out of their narrowness and selfishness, but always in the way that binds men together instead of separating them. It does not crush the flax, it does not snuff out the candle; it rather comforts the discouraged in such a way that they are once again challenged, and it challenges the complacent in such a way that they are encouraged and reassured.

It engages in these two roles of prophet and therapist more by the deeds to which it is committed than by the words it speaks. The local Church, I think, is somewhat less concerned about "going on record" or "taking a stand" than it is about deeds and actions. Its members are far more likely to challenge others by their own activities than by issuing proclamations or denunciations—much less signing a petition; and

126

they are also far more likely to encourage others by their personal commitment than they are by stirring up antagonism against some supposed "establishment."

Just as most of our current local Christian communities would not score very high on any measure either of agility or intimacy, so, too, we could not, I think, give them very many points on their transparency, their prophecy, or their healing. And yet one would hesitate to say that the small and informal Christian communities that are springing up around the land would score very much higher.

For many of these latter groups are as opaque, as narrow, as turned-in, as self-centered and self-satisfied, as harsh and judgmental as the most traditional of the traditional parishes. To make matters worse, their members are so filled with their own gnostic and elite sense of self-righteousness that they are not even aware of the beam in their own eye. There is no reason why a small community should become any more transparent, any more healing or any more challenging (in the Christian sense of the word) than a large community; it is very much easier for a small community to become narrow and "parochial" than for a larger community.

It is not my purpose to criticize the small group movements in the Church. Quite the contrary, I think they are one of the sources of great vitality and promise in American Catholicism. But simply because they are small, and simply because their members define themselves as liberal, does not at all guarantee that those looking at them from the outside will see the love which is supposed to mark the followers of Jesus of Nazareth. In fact what outsiders may frequently see is simply a more highly articulate version of distrust and suspicion.

Even though some of those ideologues who see no difference between the clergy and laity would deny it, there isn't much reason to question the fact that the leader of the local church is the one most responsible for engendering the required qualities in that church. If the leader is not agile, if he is not capable of intimacy, if his commitments and convictions are not transparent, if he is not able to combine prophecy with healing, then there isn't much reason to think his community will be much different from what he is. Perhaps the most critical difference between the ideal local Christian community and the reality that we can presently observe is that in the ideal community (or anything even remotely approaching the ideal) we will require a much higher quality and a far more intense dedication in the leadership.

The Eschatological Community

The final characteristic of the ideal local Church is that it must be eschatological. The Christian religion is one that exists in time, indeed in the "time between the times." Unlike the archaic religions it does not see man re-enacting the great events of the age of the gods. Unlike the Greek religion it does see reality as an endless series of cycles. On the contrary, it sees the human history with a beginning and an end, and while it is rooted in the remembrance of great religious experiences out of the past, such as Sinai and Calvary, it also looks forward to great events that are yet to come.

It believes in the promise in the Old Testament of the messianic banquet, of the age when God's power will overcome evil and good will reign triumphant. It believes that Jesus will return even as He has departed, and that in the "time between the times," it is our task to prepare the way for the parousia. The local community, then, of the Christian Church looks both to the past and the future. It is quite conscious of the tension and the strain between the past and the future, of its obligation both to commemorate and anticipate. Unlike its early Christian predecessors it does not expect Jesus to return immediately, and yet it realizes however long we must wait, there is not enough time to do the things that must be done. The eschatological local Church is caught in a sense of urgency; it realizes that it has little time, and that it must work feverishly while there still is time, for it is conscious that Jesus will return, and it awaits that day with both eager expectation and an almost frantic awareness of all that must yet be done.

The Christian eschatology not only awaits the Jesus who is to return, the Omega Point that is yet to come, it is also highly conscious of a Jesus who is present in our midst, of the Omega Point that is already among us.

And here, perhaps, is the secret of all the other qualities which should mark the grass-roots community of Christians. For if it is conscious of the

130

presence of Jesus, particularly the eucharistic assembly, but whenever it is gathered together in His name, profoundly, vividly, passionately aware of His presence, it will have no trouble being flexible and agile, intimate and transparent, prophetic and healing. If Jesus is in our midst we know that we must travel light, and constantly be tuned in on the promptings of the Spirit. If He is with us we know that we must love one another even as He has loved us, or His presence is rejected by our failure to love. If we are conscious that the parousia is going on even now, then the strength of our convictions, the depth of our commitments, and the joy of our faith will pour out so vigorously that no one in the world about will have any doubts as to where we stand. And if we are conscious of the witness of Jesus within us, then we will know instinctively when to comfort, when to challenge, how to prophesy and how to heal. We await eagerly, of course, the fullness of Time, the Completion of All Things, but we also know that He who completes and He who fulfills is not off in the distance but is in our midst.

One hardly needs to be told that the Christian communities that most of us are familiar with are something less than eschatological. Instead of the return of Jesus it is the return of the school children the community awaits at the end of the summer. Instead of the presence of Jesus there seems to be more concern about the presence of the parish debt. These comments are both easy and somewhat cynical, and as I have said previously, I am opposed neither to parochial schools nor to elaborate parochial structures. I do not believe that smallness of size nor simplicity of structure is necessarily any more productive of authentic Christian witness in the local community than are the parishes we presently have. But however much we may be prepared to admit in theory that neither the parish school nor the parish debt ought to get in the way of our awareness of the Omega yet to come and already in our midst, in actual concrete reality we must concede that the school and the plant have become ends and not means.

I have argued that the signs of the local Christian Church demanded more of the leader of the local Church than anyone else. Above all the eschatological awareness of the parochial community depends upon its priest. He is the one, and I suppose in the final analysis the only one, who can distinguish between ends and means, who can communicate to his colleagues the eschatological sense. It therefore follows that the priest, the leader of the local Church, must be visibly conscious of the eschatological dimensions of his life. He must have a sense of urgency, a feeling that there is not enough time, a restlessness in the face of the nonessentials, and an impatience with means turned into ends. All of this must of course be done with the healing style that we have argued is essential to the Christian community. It is not easy to combine eschatology with healing, yet at the very core of the Christian religion is the symbol which sees the eschatological Son of Man as also the suffering servant. The Christian parish, then, prepares for the return of the Son of Man precisely by serving; and its leader, its priest, communicates his own eschatological sense precisely by his ability to be a patient servant. Neither this small group parish nor the old ethnic immigrant parish has any monopoly on eschatological sense or eschatological leaders. Unfortunately, in neither type of community does one detect much sense of urgency. The complacency of the small group is different from the complacency of the large group, but it is complacency just the same. Long sideburns, however praiseworthy they may be, do not make a man an eschatologist.

But if we do not have much eschatological sensitivities, it does not mean that we cannot have such sensitivities; it only means that we haven't got them yet.

Springtime Religion

The Jewish feast of Passover is a combination of two ancient spring rites: the feast of the unleavened bread is basically an agricultural feast while the feast of the yearling lamb is the feast of a pastoral people. The former was the spring festival of the more settled Jewish tribes while the latter was the celebration of those tribes which still led a nomadic life when the tribes began to merge into the Jewish people. The linking of these combined feasts with the covenant of Sinai was in fact the conversion of a pre-covenant feast to a post-covenant meal.

But it was not a completely arbitrary conversion.

The Sinai covenant represented the beginning of a new life for the Jewish people, not merely a life free from the slavery of Egypt, not even just the promise of the new life in a land of Canaan, but most especially a new life as God's chosen people with a special messianic vocation, though the full implications of that vocation would be developed only as the centuries went on. The celebration of Easter during the springtime, then, is not merely an historical accident, but one heavily laden with religious symbolism. The spring feast of the Church represents not just a new life of freedom for the new Israel; it also represents the messianic mission of the new people of God. Even though spring comes only at a particular season of the year, the Church is a springtime organization all year round because it has the messianic mission of bringing a new life of freedom, hope and joy to the rest of the world. For Christians it is always spring, it is always the beginning of a new life, it is always the end of the harsh winter cold and the beginning of warmth and budding greenery on trees and splashes of flower color in our garden.

It therefore follows that Christians should be springtime people, people whose lives represent the same kind of symbolism that did the feast of the yearling lamb or of the unleavened bread. A Christian must live in such a way that those around him know that there is new life, new hope, new warmth, new opportunity no matter what the season of the year.

There is no better capsule summary of the ministry of Christianity than to say we are a people with a springtime vocation who have not yet been able to lead springtime lives. We are called to warmth and frequently represent coldness; we are called to represent vitality and growth and so frequently we would rather stand for sterility and drabness. We are supposed to lead the way in fresh beginnings but so frequently we choose to stand for stale conclusions. We ought to bring color and sparkle to the world but much of the time we choose rather to be sober and somber.

How many rectories, how many convents, how many schools, how many parishes are springtime communities? On the contrary, does not one often encounter in these Christian institutions, an autumn frost or a winter chill even when it is spring in the rest of the world?

Why have we chosen to be winter people when we have a springtime mission? The reason, one fears, is painfully obvious. To be a springtime person means to take risks, to open oneself up much as does a blossoming flower. There are no blossoms and no risks in the life of a winter person and while he may not be very happy, neither is there any chance of his suffering any great pains of rejection. The Lord may want us to be Passover people but we have so cleverly

136

avoided most of the other things that He has asked of us that it takes rather little ingenuity to avoid this part of our mission, too. It is then relatively simple for us to blame the lack of response to the Christian message on the hardness of heart of those to whom the message is preached. We conveniently forget that our warmth is supposed to melt the hearts of their hearts. Alas, there are not too many people avoiding the Roman Church now on the ground that there is too much springtime warmth in it.